Marilyn

Monroe

The True Story of an
American Icon

Kate Holborn

Table of Contents

Introduction

The Most Humble Of Beginnings

A Husband Too Ordinary

A Model Career

Life at Twentieth Century Fox

A Taste Of Columbia

A Series Of Ever Bigger Breaks

Rejoining Twentieth Century

Marriage To A Baseball Legend

Professional Success, Personal Heartbreak

The Intellectual Playwright and the 'Dumb Blonde'

The Final Scenes

'A candle in the wind'

Introduction

Let's think of some of our preconceptions of Marilyn Monroe.

Dumb blonde. Hollywood misfit. Calculating diva who manipulated events for her own ends.

Think of some of the images that we associate with this icon. Sitting seductively, her legs tucked under her, lips semi pouted. Or, that rolling, sexy walk.

Perhaps most famous of all, standing with mock innocence, her dress billowing up from the wind coming from the air vent below.

We should know by now that there is a difference between a screen persona and a real person, but with somebody such as

Marilyn Monroe it is difficult to separate the two.

We know her through her excesses, and through those images that are seared into our cultural consciousness.

In fact, as we shall see in this book, Marilyn was a complex character. Following a tough upbringing, she was always needy and rarely felt properly appreciated.

She was an intellectual who sought to make up for her limited education. A perfectionist who continued with acting classes even when a global star.

And she was somebody with a driving, desperate urge to succeed.

Not only succeed in her work, which was hard enough for somebody whose looks were both her making and undoing in her professional life.

But also a woman desperate to gain success in her personal relationships – and that meant not only finding love and friendship.

But also recognizing it when it was there.

The Most Humble Of Beginnings

Marilyn Monroe's connection to the movie industry started before birth. Her mother was a film cutter at Consolidated Film Industries.

Her father was…well that can only be a matter of conjecture and we will return to her parents' influence on what she would become in a short while.

On June 1st 1926, at the Los Angeles County Hospital, the tiny baby was born, and named Norma Jeane Mortenson.

Her mother named her after the silent movie idol Norma Talmadge, who was at the peak of her powers at the time young Norma was born.

In a frightening forerunner of the topsy-turvy life she would live, she did not stay a Mortenson for long.

Her name had been changed, by the time she was baptized, to Norma Jeane Baker.

The young Marilyn had a tough childhood. Her mother suffered from mental illness, and was hospitalized when her daughter was only seven.

Even before then, Marilyn had been cared for in a series of foster homes as her mother struggled to cope.

She lived for a number of years with an English couple, Ida and Albert Bolender.

But the relationship was never strong. Once, when the tiny Marilyn called Ida 'mommy', the foster mother screamed back, 'Don't you ever call me that, I'm not your mother.'

Like her mother, Marilyn's foster family were evangelical Christians, following Christian Science beliefs.

The small child was taken into care – a succession of orphanages and foster home where she was sexually assaulted, and raped at the age of eleven.

At least, that is one of the claims that Marilyn made.

Although she became more used to change, it must have been terribly disturbing for a young girl.

In some of the early occasions, she would scream and fight as she was dragged to the home, shouting that she was not an orphan.

Perhaps even more sadly, as she got older, she accepted these temporary moves as an unavoidable inevitability.

But when she had screamed that she was not an orphan, she was speaking the truth.

Both of her parents were alive, just unable (in her mother's case) and unwilling (in her father's) to look after her.

Later, she spent some time being cared for by a friend of her mother, Grace Goddard, who (along with her husband, Doc) were paid $25 per week to bring her up.

The money came from her mother, whose mental illness meant that she could not do the job herself, at least on a regular basis.

The couple were strong churchgoers, with a puritanical set of beliefs, and Marilyn's upbringing was little improved. She got on well with her foster father, but there were tensions with Grace.

When Doc's job moved him to the East Coast, in 1942, the couple could no longer afford to care for Marilyn, and she stayed behind.

Perhaps there was more to it than a lack of money. The stories were that Doc had got drunk and had tried to kiss Marilyn – but not in a loving, fatherly way.

Through the sixteen years she had lived to this point, her parents had given little to her.

That may be unfair to her mother, whose own illnesses impaired her ability to be a good role model.

Gladys Pearl Monroe Baker was just 24 years old when Marilyn was born – and by then she had already had two other children.

These were looked after by her husband, Jasper Baker, and Gladys had little or no contact with them.

Mental illness haunted her life, depression and paranoia coming and going. She once bought a house for she and Marilyn to live in, but could only manage to be there for short periods.

Gladys' own family themselves had a history of mental illness, with both her parents suffering from manic depression.

Her evangelical beliefs led her to the view that her condition was the result of an evil she had committed, and her illness was a punishment for this.

If Marilyn's relationship with her mother was extremely complex, then that with her father is easier to describe.

There simply wasn't one. In fact, the young Marilyn would often boast that her father was the actor, Clark Gable.

Apparently, there was a picture of the movie star on a wall in their house. Gladys would often tell young Marilyn, who was eager for news of her father, that he looked like the man in the photograph.

That was enough for the little girl, and she told everybody that Clark Gable was her dad.

Beyond that piece of fiction, she could only presume the identity of her father. In later life, she would describe him as a man who used to live with her mother.

But who walked out on them when she was 'getting born'.

One of two men were most likely to have been her paternal parent. These are Edward Mortenson and Stanley Gifford.

Edward Mortenson married Gladys in 1924. It is his name that is on Marilyn's birth certificate but not the name that was used when she was baptized.

Mortenson died in 1981, and when his small apartment was cleared, cuttings were found about the star, with references to her father highlighted.

However, Gladys and Edward were divorcing at the time of Marilyn's birth – the short-lived marriage had not worked out – and there was a widespread belief that another man could be the girl's biological parent.

Stanley Gifford was a work colleague of Gladys, and the two had an affair around the time of Marilyn's birth. Whether that affair had begun by the time of her conception is another matter.

However, Marilyn grew up believing that Charles Stanley Gifford (he rarely used the 'Charles') was her father.

But every approach to him was rebuffed. Growing up with such rejection must have had an impact on Marilyn's disturbed later life.

Being pushed from foster home to orphanage and back again when you have a father who will not accept his responsibilities will have cut deeply into the child's psyche.

Whether it was Mortenson, or Gifford – or even somebody else, no support was given.

Gifford became a moderately successful businessman later in his life, setting up and running a drive through diary.

Marilyn would, when she had achieved stardom, instruct her chauffeur to drive through the diary, and she would make purchases to force what she saw as her father to serve her.

She would not, however, get out of the car. Perhaps that suited both sides of the counter.

Marilyn's life took an upward turn when she entered her teens.   But then, in yet another twist, unknown circumstances dictated that she had to move out of the Goddard's home for a while.

Rather than send her back to an orphanage, she lived for a time with Grace Goddard's Aunt, Ana Lower.

The two hit it off from the outset. Aunt Ana was an active member of the Christian Science Church, and the impressionable ward followed her footsteps.

She would remain attached to the church into her early twenties, and to her 'Aunt' for much longer.

Marilyn kept a book her Aunt gave to her in later life. It was a manual instructing in the teachings of Christian Science, and contained an inscription that meant much to the girl.

It said: 'Norma dear, read this book. I do not leave you much except my love, but not even death can diminish that; nor will death ever take me far away from you.'

Aunt Ana would eventually move in with the Goddards, but by then young Marilyn (still, of course, known as Norma Jeane) was growing in confidence.

No longer was she known by school bullies as 'Norma Jeane the Human Bean.' She had been forced to repeat a year of schooling, but she progressed so much in the Eighth Grade that she was allowed to skip some of the year, and rejoin her peers.

She was able to graduate to High School – Van Nuys High School – in September 1941.

When, in 1942, her carers could not or would not take the teenager with them, she was confronted with two choices – to return yet again to an orphanage or to branch out on her own.

An option was to live again with Aunt Ana, but by this stage the lady was in her sixties, and it was feared that a move such as this would not work.

Marilyn needed love. Her mother's condition restricted a normal mother and child relationship. As we have seen, she had no stable male role model in her life.

Aunt Ana and, to a lesser extent, the Goddards had done their best, but could not replace a proper parent's love.

By now, she was a very desirable, attractive young lady.

In her mind, she found the answer to her problems. She discovered a way to find love, security and a male influence in her life.

She would find a husband.

A Husband Too Ordinary

Norma Jeane Mortenson was just eighteen days beyond her sixteenth birthday when she married the twenty-one-year-old James Dougherty.

They had known each other for a while. Marilyn may even have held a candle for the older boy.

Whilst Marilyn was living with the Goddards, their back fence marked the boundary of Dougherty's family home.

At five years older than Marilyn, Jim Dougherty would drive her to school. Travelling with them would be Doc Goddard's own daughter, Beebe.

The age gap restricted the relationship in the early days, although Marilyn might occasionally accompany Jimmy to dances and to watch movies.

But then, in 1942, the Goddards were to move. Some accounts claim that there was a specific reason why Marilyn did not accompany them.

Perhaps the story about a drunken Doc attempting to kiss Marilyn was true. If so, it is easy to understand why a deeply religious family might want to end the relationship with their foster child.

Grace Goddard felt it would be wise to extinguish any chance of a repeat of the inappropriate kiss. In fact, Marilyn's relationship with Doc Goddard remained strong throughout her adult life.

Perhaps this gives lie to the idea that Doc had tried to kiss her, or that she thought any more of it.

With Norma not wanting to return to the orphanage, she worked with Grace and Jim's mother, Ethel, to persuade young Jim that he should marry her once she turned sixteen.

It seemed as though this was a perfect solution to all of their problems – and Jim was happy to go along.

Norma maybe held a crush on Jim for many years, but she was still a young girl. (It depends whose story you believe.)

The Goddards may have felt some guilt about leaving Marilyn behind, and the marriage could offer a solution. At the time at least, the young girl was prepared to go along with the idea.

Whether she was old enough to make a rational, considered choice is, of course, a matter of conjecture.

Marilyn had by now moved to another High School, University in West Los Angeles. In May, she dropped out and became engaged to Jim.

It would be a very short engagement. Marriage followed within a month.

Nobody is sure whether this was just a marriage of convenience or the union of a young couple in love.

Whichever, on the 19th June 1942 they were married. The Bolanders featured amongst the guests. And, with no father showing, her Aunt Ana accompanied her down the aisle.

However, several people who might have been expected to be present were missing, and one was Marilyn's mother, Gladys, who was enduring one of her frequent episodes of depression and schizophrenia.

The others were the Goddards themselves, who did not return from their new home for the ceremony.

The marriage lasted for four years, before Marilyn initiated a divorce. By this time, she was becoming more and more involved with film studios.

Jim always maintained that there was nothing wrong with their marriage, but that the studio did not feel he was a suitable husband.

He was an ordinary man, from a humble if comfortable background. He believed that the studio felt their potential star in the making needed a husband with more of a backstory.

Or, even better, no husband at all.

He felt that the studio destroyed a happy, loving marriage in the interests of their publicity machine.

Marilyn, though, reported things somewhat differently. She later claimed that she had been forced into the marriage to ease the burden on Grace Goddard. A union in which love played a very small part.

Some years later, Jim refuted this, saying that he was a lucky man to get a bride like Marilyn, but feared that fame had turned her head.

And she had forgotten how much in love they had been.

Grace Goddard's actions in manipulating the union began to bear more greatly upon the young wife.

Although Marilyn retained a good relationship with Doc up until almost the end of her life, the same was not true with Grace.

Perhaps she felt saddened and let down too that the Grace did not attend her wedding.

During the first year of their marriage, Marilyn and Jim spent a lot of time together.

Jim recalled it as a time of fun and laughter for the young lovers.

Marilyn viewed it differently, feeling that the couple did as Jim wanted – fishing and skiing were two hobbies he loved but were of much less interest to his wife.

Only occasionally would they go to dances, or to see films – the sort of things Marilyn would choose.

Whilst Jim was loving their time together, Marilyn later claimed that she attempted suicide during these years. Something which she would attempt more than once.

Meanwhile, war had escalated in Europe, and now the USA was drawn in. Jim joined the Merchant Marines late in 1943 and the couple were moved to Catalina Island, which lies close to the coast of southern California.

Jim was a physical training instructor, and during this time Marilyn took up weight lifting. Taking care of her physique would become important to her for most of her remaining days.

Then, the following year, Jim was shipped overseas. Marilyn went to live with his mother, and took up work at the Radio Plane Company.

The Burbank based corporation operated as a defense plant, and was owned by an actor, Reginald Denny.

Marilyn was a hard worker. She was promoted out of her job of inspecting parachutes, although it was not a promotion she probably enjoyed.

She was moved to the task of spraying planes with a protective liquid plastic. The fumes were atrocious, so much so that the room became known as 'the dope room'.

However, Marilyn's work was good enough to earn her a special certificate.

A propaganda visits in 1945, however, would change her life forever.

An army photographer visited the workplace in order to take pictures of women working in support of the war effort.

He was looking for a face to promote morale for the troops stationed far away overseas in Europe.

A young girl, dressed in her company overalls, caught his attention. Norma Jeane Dougherty was that woman. They spoke, and Marilyn revealed that she had a jumper in her locker.

Pictures of girls with jumpers were in vogue at the time, and the photographer began snapping away.

The series of photographs David Conover took would appear on the cover of *Yank* magazine. Marilyn was about to embark on a new career.

She would be a model. She possessed a natural flair in front of the camera, and it responded to her, enhancing her sensuous sexuality and glorious beauty.

Her new career would provide her with a purpose in life, and get her the adoration she always believed was unattainable, Aunt Ana apart.

But it would also signal the end of her first marriage. Although still living with her in-laws, by the middle of 1945 they were becoming alarmed by their daughter in law's growing career as a model.

It was agreed that it would be a good decision – for all – for her to return to Aunt Ana for a while. A typical dispute arose as Marilyn committed full time to her modeling.

The Dougherty family thought that she should discuss this with Jim, by writing to him overseas. Marilyn felt that this would slow down her progress.

She followed her own beliefs. But when Jim returned on leave – only the second opportunity they had received to spend time together since he had been posted – he was worried by the changes he found.

A pile of unpaid bills told that she was spending their money on her career, and modeling was the only topic in which she showed much interest.

Rather than spend time with Jim, she continued to follow her modeling commitments, and headed north west for an extended shoot with another photographer, Andre de Dienes.

Jim had to come to terms with the fact that not only were they not going to do just as he wanted, as had been the case before he signed up for the forces, but that he was now peripheral to her life.

The quiet girl who had enjoyed peace and security when they first married, was now a lady with a commitment to a glamorous but demanding career.

When his leave ended, he must have realized that his marriage would also soon be over. She had used to write to him every day, but on this, his third tour of duty, she did not write to him at all.

In fact, the next he heard was from her attorney. Marilyn had moved to Nevada, and had filed for divorce.

Jim would not sign the papers, and on his return argued for their marriage, but Marilyn's mind was made up.

She would become an actress and to do that as a woman married to an ordinary man would be almost unachievable.

Given the choice between her career and her husband, there was no question which she should pursue.

Whilst more and more opportunities had arisen for Marilyn, about which we will learn in the next chapter, Jim was discharged from the navy, the war at an end.

He returned home to find a wife with new, more glamourous interests. A wife who had decided on a career path, one that offered little time for a returning husband.

Within a short period, she resumed divorce proceedings, and their marriage ended in 1946.

Although Marilyn moved on with her life, attaining worldwide stardom, Jim remained very much in love with his sweetheart. But there was nothing more he could do.

He joined the Los Angeles police force, retiring in 1974. After that, he moved to Arizona and Maine.

In the New England state, he was elected to become a County Commissioner, and taught at the Maine Criminal Justice Academy.

But he continued to think of Marilyn. He followed her life and career in close detail, an ordinary husband who lacked the glamour to be married to a Hollywood star.

In 1976, fourteen years after her death, he published a book, The Secret Happiness of Marilyn Monroe.

Another memoir followed in 1997, called To Norma Jeane With Love, Jimmie. To him, she was always Norma Jeane, and never Marilyn Monroe.

In his eighties, he appeared in a documentary, Marilyn's Man.

Jim Dougherty contracted leukemia, and complications with pneumonia followed. He died, at the age of 84, on August 15th 2005.

Jim left behind three daughters and two stepdaughters.

A Model Career

As much of a natural as Marilyn was in front of the camera, she was also a hard worker. She sought to enhance her innate ability through learning technique and demonstrating commitment.

Following the propaganda shoot with Conover, she began working freelance with him, earning $5 a time.

Not a bad bit of pocket money for the young wife. But nothing like the monies she would earn in the future.

As for Conover himself, he worked as an official army photographer, operating through the Hal Roach Studios.

The commanding officer to whom Conover reported was a certain Ronald Reagan. Marilyn began to appear in other publications – still those connected to the military – such as the magazine *Stars and Stripes*.

She went on a lengthy shoot with him through southern California. There was something about Marilyn before a camera.

Perhaps it was a look that said, 'Protect Me', something she may have developed as a child. She was, after all, an extremely vulnerable person.

Others feel that she always had in mind modeling as a stepping stone to a more lucrative future – in the movies.

The next step in her career came when a commercial photographer, Potter Hueth, saw some of Conover's photos.

He saw the potential in her, and asked her to have some photographs taken that he could show around.

If they got bought, she would be paid, if not, then it would go down to experience.

Marilyn was keen to advance her career and agreed. However, she could only pose in the evenings, her work at the defense plant occupying her during the day.

These early photographs are interesting to view from today's perspective. They portray an innocence, a cheeriness below which are hints of sadness.

She is undoubtedly beautiful, but the camera captures that vulnerability, and she seems to call out for love.

Hueth's photographs somehow found their way to the desk of an agency, the Blue Book Model Agency, which operated out of Los Angeles.

The head of the company was Emmeline Snively, and she recognized something in the photographs, and was intrigued. She wrote to Marilyn, offering her a contract.

But she would need to pay $100 for a modeling course beforehand. However, the fee could come out of her earnings, and Marilyn took the next step on her career.

Her first job, though, was not in front of a camera. An industrial show was due to start at the Pan Pacific Auditorium, and Holga Steel had a stand.

She was hired to be a hostess for them. However, she continued to attend her modeling classes, and was taught how to improve her smile.

It was during her time with Snively that her name changed yet again. Norma Jeane was considered too ordinary for certain assignments, and she would adopt the name Jean Norman.

Marilyn continued to study hard. She was self-critical, and would ask what she had done wrong in the photographs she felt were not as successful.

She was also a quick learner, and rarely made the same mistake twice.

Marilyn's natural hair color was brown, with natural kinks giving it body. With an assignment for shampoo to be photographed in an evening, she took advice on how she could look even better.

Stars such as Rita Hayworth and Ingrid Bergman used Frank and Joseph's Beauty Salon, and Marilyn was sent there.

Nervously, she asked what could be done. Her hair was straightened, and color applied. The result was a reddish blonde look, which she really liked.

From there, Marilyn had her hair dyed even blonder, sure that it set off her eyes to better effect.

The image that would become iconic before too long was beginning to take shape. Some reports say that she did not want to become a blonde, but according to her stylist, that was the opposite to the truth.

In terms of her life's timeline, it was around this point that she divorced Jim. Her modeling career was booming, and she was earning a strong reputation as a big attraction for men's magazines.

She did not possess the tall, slender looks for fashion modeling, but as a pin up she was perfect. She began to appear in numerous publications.

These included *Peek*, *See*, *Glamorous Models*, *Cheesecake* and *US Camera*. The names of the magazines offer a big clue as to their style and content!

They did not show nude pictures, but the models would be scantily clad and suggestively posed. Although the magazines raised eyebrows in some quarters, it was all extremely innocent by modern standards.

Amongst the photographers with whom she worked was the aforementioned Andre de Dienes, with whom she collaborated from the end of the war to 1949.

The often traveled together, shooting in Nevada, the Mojave Desert and Oregan. A session in the Yosemite in the winter of 1945 led to a famous collection of the young Norma Jeane taming the untamed world of the Pacific coast.

Marilyn and de Dienes fell in love, and at one stage she agreed to marry him but he moved away from Los Angeles, and she would not follow to another city. Her future, she was sure, lay in the movies, and that meant Hollywood.

Despite the allure of the modeling world, it was not lucrative, and Marilyn would often struggle for money, although another photographer, Earl Moran, gave her work in those years.

Some of his pictures were semi-nude. Marilyn often felt that the work he offered kept her going before her breakthrough in the movies.

At the same time, just as others who worked with her believed, he said that she was a natural in front of the camera, able to exploit her sexiness and with a reputation for throwing herself fully into the pictures.

Marilyn's commitment to a career in modeling during the 1940s was, though, part of a plan. She always intended to end up in the movies, taking the trouble to have a screen test as early as 1945.

Blue Book's Emmeline Snively would once again play a major part in her career development as she brought her to the attention of Hollywood producers.

When Marilyn returned home to the West following her divorce, Snively had planted a little snippet of news with the gossip columnists.

The millionaire Howard Hughes was in hospital at the time, following a flying accident. Snively planted the idea that the medicine that set him on the road to recovery was not some new-fangled drug.

No, it was the sight of Norma Jeane Dougherty in a magazine that got his blood pumping healthily once more.

The extent to which Hughes was caught by the young model is open to argument, but he did send an aide to inquire further about her.

It was enough for Snively to appoint an agent for her model – that was Helen Ainsworth of the National Concert Artists Corporation.

Matters were beginning to become interesting.

Ainsworth passed on her protégé to another agent, Harry Lipton, and he organized a meeting with the Fox casting director, Ben Lyon.

Lyon realized that, despite her naivete, the young girl before him had set her mind on being an actress. Whilst others might get up to all sorts with movie moguls and directors, it was clear that she was not that sort of girl.

He saw something of Jean Harlow in Marilyn. That actress too had possessed an innate sexiness, a natural affinity with the camera.

His own background in film showed him that what she lacked in experience, she made up for in her charm and charisma.

And these would be magnified on the big screen.

She undertook a screen test – unusually for the time, it was in color. This to show off her charms to the maximum.

Within a week, it was seen by Darryl Zanuck, head of production at Fox, and Marilyn had a contract.

She would be paid $75 a week for six months.

She had been married, separated and by now almost divorced. She had been the pin up on the cover magazines, and now she was about to become a movie star.

All this, and she was just twenty years of age.

Another change was about to occur. Lyon loved his new discovery, but thought that the name Norma Jeane Dougherty was not the moniker of a movie star.

He recalled an actress from the 1920s of whom he was a fan – Marilyn Miller. In turn, Marilyn thought of her own mother's family name – Monroe.

Goodbye Norma Jeane, and hello to Marilyn Monroe.

Meanwhile, Gladys had just been returned to a mental asylum, and could not celebrate her daughter's success.

In fact, despite the excitement of the contract and new name, fame and glory would take longer to come about than her daughter would ever have expected or dreamt.

And many would say that the latter of those two abstract nouns, 'glory', would always remain just beyond her fingertips.

Life at Twentieth Century Fox

Despite her contract with Twentieth Century Fox, any dreams of stardom had to be put on hold.

Marilyn's life was devoted to singing and dancing classes. She spent her time with other newly contracted actors and actresses, honing her skills.

With her experience and talent for posing for stills, she was often the subject of publicity shots, bringing a sparkle and energy to a subject that few others could match.

It was not just her name that was changed. Fox sought to create a whole back biography for Marilyn, a more romantic one that had been her real life.

This fictional account said that she had been discovered after babysitting for a talent scout employed by the studios.

If progress with Fox was steady but slow, Marilyn went out of her way to milk any opportunity with the press.

This included donning a bathing costume and reporting for duty on a beach one morning. Not too extreme, it might be thought, until it is realized that this shoot took place on a cold November day.

She gained favor amongst reporters, many of whom were permanently based at the studios. They awarded her the title 'Miss Press Club' in 1948.

Sidney Skolsky was one such reporter. He wrote a well-known entertainment column which was widely read and respected.

It was even claimed a great review from Sidney could make a star, whilst a bad one could end a career. He became friends with Marilyn, and remained so throughout the remainder of her life.

When the press turned, after she became famous, Sidney was one of the few who stayed by her side.

Like many before him, he was won over by her determination to succeed. He noted that she was committed to improvement, and had a rare drive – and need – to make it to the big time.

Whilst her training continued, she began to get parts as extras in films. Although she would not even appear in credits, and had no lines, she was beginning to learn the trade of the movie actress.

Then, in 1947, came her next break. *Scudda Hoo! Scudda Hay!* – it is not a film which has particularly stood the test of time, but it gave Marilyn her first line on the big screen.

She appears paddling a canoe in the movie, which is a musical comedy about two brothers battling to get their girl. But her line comes in another scene, where she walks down the steps of a church.

In full close up she announces her immortal words - 'Hi, Rad'. Unfortunately, whilst the line remains, the close up ended its life on the cutting room floor.

The film also sees the debut of another actress who would meet an early end – Natalie Wood.

Unfortunately for Marilyn, but perhaps unsurprisingly, *Scudda* did not see her immediately paddling off to starring roles.

Later, she met Joseph Schneck, a founder of Fox and at the time an executive producer. He was seventy by this time but the two became friends, and Marilyn was often invited to dinner parties at his house.

Some stories circulated later that she had been his mistress, but if so, she did not do it for her career. That continued to flounder along, like a holed canoe.

But her friendship with Schneck continued, and she visited him on his deathbed in 1961, just a year before she would die herself.

She cried after the meeting. Far more likely than a sexual relationship is that Schneck was an interesting storyteller, who could teach Marilyn much about the workings of the industry.

And, perhaps, offered the father figure she still craved.

Her next 'break' came in the movie *Dangerous Years*, which was a serious film about juvenile delinquency in post-war America.

This time her close up materialized, and she was given a billing on the credits.

But that was followed by disappointment. Fox, who had used more for publicity than acting, ended her contract.

However, Marilyn used this setback as an opportunity to widen her career. She won second lead at a Beverley Hills theatre (the Bliss Hayden Miniature Theatre) in a play called *Glamour Preferred*.

The theatre often featured young hopefuls, and was known as a ground in which those with potential could be spotted and snapped up. As well as Marilyn, other stars who performed there included Doris Day and Debbie Reynolds.

A Taste Of Columbia

Following a short spell contracted to MGM, as a result of a friendship developed with a talent scout there, Joseph Schneck gave her a giant helping hand.

After speaking with the head of the Columbia Studios, Harry Cohn, she was offered a contract with the industry giant.

The other friendships she had engendered along the way, and her commitment and work ethic no doubt helped her as well.

At this time, Marilyn was not only honing her acting skills, but also her mind. Her education had been patchy, and she was determined to catch up.

After all, acting is about empathy, and she needed to understand the character she would play in the roles that she was given.

It was while she was at Columbia that tragic news reached her. Her Aunt Ana died. Marilyn later said that her Aunt had always believed in her, and was the first person she had properly loved.

She appeared in only one film for Columbia, but she did take the second lead. In *Ladies of the Chorus* she played a stage star who falls in love with the son of a wealthy family.

The film was a low budget musical, but it did mark her biggest role to date.

The musical director of the film was Fred Karger, and he assisted Marilyn with her voice development.

The two became every closer and began dating. During this spell, Marilyn found that she belonged. Karger's family welcomed her into their clan.

His mother, Anne (everyone called her Nana) was a part of the glory years of the 1920s in Hollywood, having a permanent suite at the Hollywood Hotel, where she used to hold open houses for the like of Rudolph Valentino and Jack Pickford.

Marilyn wanted to take the relationship with her voice coach further, but it had been just a pleasant distraction to Karger, and they split.

However, she stayed close to Nana, learning from the lady's great experience.

Along with the help given to her voice, she also received support for her acting, from

Columbia's head of drama coaching, Natasha Lytess. She recognized that Marilyn had the potential to be more than just a pretty face.

She also recognized her drive to succeed, and her determination to take every opportunity to improve her skills.

Despite these positive steps in her career, in general, her experiences at Columbia were not good, and for this she blamed the mogul Harry Cohn, Columbia's chief.

He was famous for his volatile nature, and she claimed that he ditched her from his studio after she refused to spend a weekend on his yacht.

She may have been prepared to do almost anything to further her career, but there were limits.

A Series Of Ever Bigger Breaks

Lean times followed her release from Columbia. Although she retained support of her agent, Harry Lipton, and friends she had made, finding jobs was difficult.

She tried to return to modeling, but even here it was tricky to find work.

Then, she got a small break. The Marx Brothers were coming to the end of their careers, but released a film called *Love Happy*.

Marilyn earned a bit part in it, where she walked with her trademark rock and roll past one of the brothers.

It was a tiny role in a flop of a film. But it got her noticed.

However, before it was released, she agreed to do something that would stay with her forever. That was to appear in a nude photo shoot for a calendar.

The two iconic pictures – one of her lying full length, the other sitting up with her legs tucked under her – were enormous hits, but she was only paid $50 for the session.

When *Love Happy* was released, a big Hollywood agent, Johnny Hyde, was impressed, and agreed with Harry Lipton to take her on.

It would prove to offer a much-needed push in her work.

As executive vice president of the well-regarded William Morris Agency, Hyde oozed class, and Marilyn was impressed immediately.

He had worked with the mega stars of Hollywood – Guy Madison, Howard Keel and Rita Hayworth amongst them. Despite ill health, he made it his goal to promote Marilyn's career.

He also fell in love with her, but whilst she liked the man, she determined to keep the relationship professional.

He organized for her to have a small amount of plastic surgery, to make her already stunning looks even more perfect. He ensured that the best hairdressers looked after her.

And he arranged for her to audition for the role in the hard-hitting drama, directed by John Huston, *The Ashphalt Jungle*.

Her audition was stunning, and Huston decided to cast her immediately. She was playing the role of Angela Phinlay, a crooked lawyer's mistress. It would be her first major role in a leading film.

She received critical acclaim for her performance, and had proved that she could be a serious actress.

Huston's genius is legendary. In this piece he demonstrated a deep understanding of Marilyn's talents.

Her character is not evil, but has the mixture of sensuality and innocence that would drive a man wild. That was what she brought to the screen.

It was a complex performance from a complex lady, but one who had finally demonstrated that she was more than just a pin up with a pretty face and superb body.

Although the starring role was still eluding her, Marilyn was beginning to pick up work. She appeared in a film about industry, a TV commercial and a couple of bit parts, including one with Mickey Rooney.

But her next giant leap, under the tutelage of Johnny Hyde, was to appear in Joseph Mankiewicz's *All About Eve*.

This film, which cast a jaundiced eye over life in the theatre, was a critical success, and although her role was a little smaller than in

The Ashphalt Jungle, it was another achievement on her growing resume.

In *All About Eve,* she played the role of Miss Caswell, a talentless actress who openly uses her body and looks to get parts.

Rejoining Twentieth Century

Her role in *All About Eve* saw another chance offered at 20th Century Fox.

She auditioned opposite the actor Richard Conte, who found her a serious and committed actress, with a natural style.

She was immediately offered a contract. As good news as this was for Marilyn, it was also tinged with sadness. Johnny Hyde, who had steered her through the complex roads to near stardom, died.

His already weak heart gave way, and he suffered a major coronary. Marilyn was heart-broken, and entered a bout of depression. She went to stay with the acting coach Natasha Lytess, who was by now working regularly with her.

Whilst there, she took an overdose of sleeping pills, her second attempt at suicide.

She was soon back at work with Fox, and was offered a role in the comedy *As Young as You Feel.*

Her role as Harriet, a heartless secretary, was originally quite small but such was Marilyn's growing reputation that it grew, and gained her rave notices following strong box office returns.

In 1951, she began to believe that she had finally arrived. Not only was she pictured, in color, in *Life* magazine, but she was invited to present an Oscar at the Academy Awards.

Whilst mostly popular, any attractive and successful lady is likely to promote jealousy. Told by a journalist that she wore sluttish clothes and would look better in a potato sack, she was pictured wearing one.

It was a lovely touch of self-irony.

She even received a sack of potatoes from a farm for promoting the vegetable, albeit inadvertently.

The head of Fox, Darryl Zanuck, saw that he had a potential source of profit on his hands. Marilyn received more requests for photos than any other star in his stable.

He felt that he could exploit this for profit, and began casting her in a series of films in which she was typecast as the dumb blonde.

This character would nearly always be both stupid, but attractive.

For an actress who had a good range and saw herself as serious, this must have been disappointing, but her hard upbringing had made her nothing if not pragmatic. She took the roles.

These days, actors do anything to avoid becoming typecast. In allowing herself to do so, Marilyn made one of the first mistakes to her burgeoning reputation. A mistake that would haunt her for much of her career.

Some of the films, though, were good, and did reasonably well at the box office, *As Young as You Feel* was a case in point.

But others simply regurgitated the stock characterization. After a while, she began to tire of these roles in low budget films.

Then, before she knew it, she was awarded a seven-year contract. Something unheard of for a still little-known actress.

This followed her turning up for a Hollywood party late. With all the big stars of the day present, and a large press attendance, she arrived, out of breath in a stunning strapless dress.

The press descended, leaving more established stars behind, and demanded to know which movies she would soon be in.

Fox realized that it had the potential of a major movie star on its hands.

Through the early fifties, her career rose and rose. Instead of causing outrage with her nude photos, she gained public support; when it emerged that her mother was in a mental asylum, Marilyn came out smelling of roses.

The story had always been that her parents were dead, but Marilyn told the truth, explaining that the lies were to protect her mother from a spotlight she would be unable to handle.

She then moved her mother to a private home.

She became big enough to have her own manager, but still worked hard on her acting skills, studying for a time with the method actor Martin Checkov.

Following an operation for appendicitis, she appeared again in *Life* magazine, the seriousness of her interests – a bookcase full of intellectual books on Fabianism, discrimination and the history of the theatre contrasting with the sex bomb image

She became the soldier's pin up, with a whole battalion stationed in Korea asking to marry her. She received up to 5000 letters per week.

The opportunity of a serious part then arose. She would, for the first time, play the lead in a piece of proper drama.

In *Don't Bother to Knock*, she was cast as a disturbed babysitter who endangers a girl left in her care.

Although her co-star Anne Bancroft talked up Marilyn's performance, saying it moved her to tears, unfortunately the film received poor notices, in particular Monroe, who was accused of being melodramatic.

However, another meaty role soon followed. She was cast as Rose Loomis, a scheming woman who seeks to have her husband murdered.

The character uses her blatant sex appeal to manipulate the men in her life, and the film, *Niagara* (it was filmed against the backdrop of the spectacular Falls) was a popular success.

It made over $6 million at the box offices.

Marilyn Monroe – Hollywood star

Marilyn was now an established star. She outfought the, by now fading, legend Betty Grable for the role of the said blonde in the hit *Gentlemen Prefer Blondes.*

She earned a little under $20000 for her role in the film – a fortune for a girl from a poor background who had survived on bits and pieces for most of her career.

But this was still a fraction of the cost to the studio of hiring a name such as Grable.

Jane Russell co-starred in the production, and the two became friends. But although Marilyn had, with this film, demonstrated that she had arrived, her time keeping was becoming a problem.

The previously determined, committed girl began to show up late for filming. In fact, there was nothing to do with laziness, or her success going to her head, in this. Marilyn was simply very nervous.

She had to spend time preparing herself to face the day ahead. It was only with the help of her new-found friend, Jane Russell, that Marilyn managed to get through filming.

Russell talked her through sessions, instilling confidence back into her.

Howard Hawks, the director, was known for not tolerating the whims of his actors, and the set became a place of tension.

He must, though, have recognized Marilyn's talents – not only had he cast her in this film but was also the director of a slightly earlier of her pieces, *Monkey Business*.

In the musical comedy, *Gentlemen Prefer Blondes*, Marilyn's character Lorelei sings the hit number, *Diamonds are a Girl's Best Friend*.

Once again, the film was a popular success. The critics, though, were mixed in their views, many of them overlooking Marilyn's acting skills for a focus on her looks.

As much as Marilyn appreciated praise for her beauty, it was faint praise. She would much prefer recognition of her talents as an actress.

Despite any lingering doubts from the men of the press, she had made it. Following

Gentlemen Prefer Blondes a host of awards was showered on her.

These included Best Young Box Office Personality from the women's magazine, *Redbook*. Most Promising Female Newcomer was then awarded to her from the *Look* periodical.

When she was awarded Fastest Rising Star of 1952 by the Photoplay organization, the dress she wore to collect it was so sensational that actor Jerry Lewis supposedly leaped on to his table, whooping his approval.

Unfortunately, the jealousy she had occasionally witnessed raised its head at this event.

Joan Crawford implied that her behavior was un-ladylike; others reported that she was taking her sexuality too far.

She and Jane Russell also got to leave their handprints and footprints in the cement outside a Hollywood theatre, a sign that a star had been accepted by the profession.

Marilyn joked that an imprint of her bottom and Jane Russell's breasts might have been more appropriate than their hands and feet.

All was going well for Marilyn. Despite nerves and jealousy, she was the star she had always dreamt of becoming.

Her love life was on the up as well.

Marriage To A Baseball Legend

Before she met Joe Dimaggio for the first time, Marilyn had some pre-conceptions regarding sports stars.

She was not a fan herself, and saw these athletes as loud, bullish competitors who would expect to get their own way.

She could not have been more wrong when it came to Joe DiMaggio.

Joltin' Joe, as he was known, was a quiet, almost reticent man. He was born in Martinez, California in 1914 and his father was a fisherman.

DiMaggio later recalled attempting anything to get out of cleaning his father's boat, with its stink of fish and remains.

He got his baseball break when his brother, who played for San Francisco Seals, talked the coach into giving his younger sibling a chance.

He moved to the New York Yankees after recovering from a career-threatening injury, making his debut in 1936. He was known at the club as the 'Yankee Clipper' for his sleek, athletic fielding.

His fame was ensured following a record-breaking 56 game hitting run. He had already been married once, and had a son, when he met Marilyn.

DiMaggio had recently retired from the Yankees, and his meeting with Marilyn was organized by a friend.

The baseball legend arrived at the date wearing a sober suit and a polka dot tie – completely not what Marilyn had expected. She said that he looked more like a 'Congressman' than a sports player.

DiMaggio was a shy man, and the lifestyle of a movie star was anathema to him, but he was taken by Marilyn and pressured for another date. She would eventually give in.

But despite the feelings he held for her, the relationship was rocky from the outset. Natasha Lytess was still a major influence in Marilyn's life, and she did not warm to DiMaggio.

For his part, he could not understand why anybody would want to be involved in such a snide, cut-throat business as the film industry.

But their relationship progressed. For Marilyn, she was growing daily in the business, and getting the media attention that followed.

Trivia began to invade her life; the press reported that she arrived at a party by helicopter. She was photographed at a pageant posing with women from the armed services.

But her low-cut dress tempted the photographers to take ever more risqué pictures until an officer stepped in and killed the photographs.

He was afraid that the reputation of the army would suffer.

It was a relatively unimportant matter, but was blown out of proportion and became front page news after the photos were leaked to the press.

DiMaggio was uncomfortable with all the attention, and also with Marilyn's willingness to teasingly exploit it for her career. He found the focus on her sexuality uncomfortable and inappropriate.

Despite a rocky courtship, however, the couple were married on January 14th, 1954.

The tried to keep the wedding date quiet, but the press were still there in number. The couple went to Japan for their honeymoon and were greeted by swarms of fans.

Such was the intensity of the crowd that the newly-weds were forced to return to their plane and exit through the baggage hatch.

The Japanese press went to town. Marilyn had superstar status in the country, mostly for her sensuous performances.

She was asked if she slept in the nude, if she wore underwear and whether she had read the Kinsey report of female sexuality.

The quiet DiMaggio was outraged. Later in the honeymoon she met a senior army officer, who asked if she would perform to troops in nearby Korea. She agreed, against the wishes of DiMaggio who thought the enterprise would be dangerous.

When a few months after their return Marilyn traveled to New York to film *The*

Seven Year Itch, DiMaggio did not initially accompany her.

Tensions within the marriage had been growing. Her husband was becoming increasingly angered with Marilyn's roles just being of the blonde bombshell variety.

When DiMaggio did eventually join her in the east, matters deteriorated even further.

He witnessed what is probably the most iconic moment of her career, the wind in the skirt scene.

Such was the media and public interest as Billy Wilder tried to direct the moment, that he offered that Marilyn would pose for them if they allowed him to finish the take.

DiMaggio would utter the immortal line 'What the hell's going on here?' as he walked in to see his wife paraded before 2000 members of the public.

The filed for divorce a short time later. Even the separation was played out in front of a frenzied media, who exploited their real-life soap opera for every penny.

If her first marriage was destroyed because the film industry thought her husband too bland, the second was ruined because Marilyn was seen as not bland enough.

Professional Success, Personal Heartbreak

Whilst her personal life was in ruin, Marilyn's professional life appeared to be at its peak.

But whilst this was how her loving public perceived matters, Marilyn herself seemed less happy. Perhaps, given the turbulent relationship with her baseball playing lover, this can be understood.

Prior to meeting DiMaggio, she had starred with Lauren Bacall and Betty Grable in *How to Marry a Millionaire*.

Despite anticipation from the press, she got on well with her co-stars, especially Grable. There was no bad feeling over their rivalry for the part of Lorelei in *Gentlemen Prefer Blondes*.

Next, with her star still on a rise, she was cast in *River of No Return*. But this did not achieve the same level of success.

Co-starring with Robert Mitchell, she fell out with Australian director Otto Preminger, who was unhappy about the role Natasha Lycett was playing in the production.

Marilyn also injured her foot during shooting.

Even more problems occurred when she was cast, against her will, in *The Girl in Pink Tights*.

She was fed up with playing dumb blonde roles, and was even more angry that she was being underpaid.

The studio simply argued that she was on a contract, and should get on without such a fuss. But Marilyn felt the script was weak and refused to participate. On this occasion she won, and the film was never finished.

Next came an underwhelming production of *There's No Business Like Show Business*, in which she was persuaded to take a smaller role in return for being awarded the lead in *The Seven Year Itch*.

The musical revival was not a success, but Marilyn still stole the headlines with her close-cut skirts – no wonder DiMaggio was getting increasingly unhappy.

The Seven Year Itch was one of her most successful films, despite the heartache happening in the background.

But shooting was difficult, with Marilyn frequently late on set. In fact, things picked up after the announcement of her divorce. It was as though, with the details finally out in the open, a weight was lifted from her.

From there, Marilyn began to put her foot down about the number of dumb blonde roles the studio was offering.

She formed a company, partnering with a photographer – Milton Green, called Marilyn Monroe productions.

The idea was simple – they would select the films Marilyn wanted, she would star in them and Green would deal with all the finances.

Her confidence restored, she turned down a succession of films proposed to her by 20th Century Fox.

The studio responded by claiming that she had become impossible to work with. It also claimed that she could not act. (That had not stopped it offering her three contracts in total, and giving her star billing in a number of its films.)

She moved to Connecticutt, and lived for a while with Green and his wife, and there began to recover from the stresses and ordeals of Hollywood and her failed marriage.

And it was during this period that she met Arthur Miller.

The Intellectual Playwright and the 'Dumb Blonde'

Arthur Miller has been widely called the greatest dramatist of the 20th Century. An American Jew, he was a child of the Depression, deeply affected by it when his father's business collapsed.

From a state of relative affluence, Miller had to work in a warehouse to pay his way through university.

From there, he tried to make a career as a playwright, and joined the Federal Theatre Project, although Congress became concerned that it had been infiltrated by communists, and closed it down.

He worked for a while in a shipyard, whilst still writing plays, and made his breakthrough in 1947, with the searing *All My Sons*.

He followed these two years later with probably his most famous play, *Death of a Salesman*, a savage indictment of the American Dream.

When he wrote *The Crucible*, a historical play in which he drew close associations to the McCarthy witch hunts, his stature as the master wordsmith of his generation was secured.

In fact, shortly after *The Crucible* was finished, Miller appeared before the House of Un-American Activites, and refused to identify members of the Communist Party working within the arts.

Marilyn moved to New York in the summer of 1955. She had met Miller back in 1950, and had been somewhat taken with the playwright.

However, he was a married man at that time.

Marilyn spent her time in New York shopping, developing her mind, improving her serious acting skills, and dating Miller.

He divorced his first wife in 1956, and married Marilyn shortly afterward, on July 1st.

But tragedy would not leave Marilyn alone. When it leaked out that the two were planning to marry, the press went wild.

Miller took Marilyn to his country farm, in Connecticut to try to evade the press, and promised them a conference.

But like animals at feeding time, the gathered corps could not contain themselves, and in trying to get to the farm one of their group was killed in a car accident.

Marilyn was mortified.

Miller had a ready-made family, and his children took to Marilyn, who in turn idolized them. She converted to Judaism to show support and devotion to Miller by adopting his religion.

His parents also became close to her, and Marilyn remained particularly attached to his father – perhaps he represented a figure that had always been absent from her life.

Soon after this, Marilyn and her new husband flew to London to film her new role, which would be a serious and challenging part.

In fact, she would be directed by, and star opposite, Laurence Olivier in his production of *The Prince and the Showgirl*.

But the differences between the classical actor and the young star were too great. Marilyn found him intimidating, and lost confidence quickly.

With echoes back to her mother, and grandmother, she became neurotic and was unable to sleep.

Miller spent many hours trying to calm and reassure her, but the shoot was a disaster.

However, the film itself was considered a success. Perhaps the vulnerability that marked her best-regarded pieces was more pronounced than in other films – after all it was a time when she was extremely vulnerable.

She also provides a strong contrast for Olivier's theatrical style. The character was perfectly suited to her.

Not only is her character, Elsie Marina, always late, but she has a child-like innocence which is extremely fetching.

Marilyn's performance went on to win Italy's David di Donatello Prize for Best Foreign Actress, as well as France's Crystal Star Award for the same achievement.

Miller continued to work on *The Misfits*, and other stories, and Marilyn slowed down in her schedule.

Although their lives seemed happily entwined again, three events occurred which serve to demonstrate that Marilyn would never find true happiness.

Firstly, Miller was found guilty of contempt of court for his performance to Congress. He was furious, and spent over a year getting the decision overturned. It caused much stress in their household.

And Marilyn split acrimoniously from her business partner, Milton Green.

Then, in June 1957, she became pregnant. Initially thrilled, her joy turned to horror as the pregnancy had to be terminated.

She fell into depression. She became more dependent on sleeping pills. She attempted suicide once more.

Her next film was Billy Wilder's *Some like it Hot*. A film which would prove to be her biggest success financially.

Co-starring with Tony Curtis and Jack Lemmon, the film is a spoof gangster movie. But despite the hit it would become, Marilyn's increasingly bizarre and worrying behavior caused severe problems during production.

Not only was she increasingly and considerably dependent on sleeping pills, but she was drinking heavily as well, drifting in and out of bouts of depression.

On a good day, she would fly through takes with her previous professionalism, but these days were not common.

Her co-stars, particularly Tony Curtis, became frustrated with working with her. The director, Billy Wilder, was particularly disparaging.

With the benefit of time, however, he relented to some extent, recognizing that, as disorganized and hard work as she was, she also possessed great comic timing.

What he did not know was the Marilyn was once again pregnant but, for the girl to whom happiness just would not stick, she miscarried after filming was complete.

As frustrating as it was for others to try and work with her, she had her own demons, and both she and Miller felt that it was the pressures of the production that contributed to the loss of their baby.

The award of a Golden Globe for Best Actress in a Comedy or Musical category was of little comfort.

Such was her desire for a child of her own, that she took invasive fertility treatment, but this was unsuccessful.

Her next film was a distinctly uninspiring comedy, *Let's Make Love*. It was a return to the insipid, stock character production in which Fox seemed to specialize with regards to Marilyn.

She only agreed to do it because the other options she was offered were even worse. Miller tried a re-write, but even his genius could not lift it.

Marilyn's behavior became more unreliable and unpleasant during filming, with much of her ire aimed at her husband.

But such was the poor quality of the script, that Fox could not find a leading man to star opposite Marilyn – perhaps her growing poor reputation as somebody with whom to work added to this.

In the end the French star, Yves Montand was cast. Before long, the two were having an affair. This seemed to modify her on set behaviour, and worked well with the rest of the cast.

The affair ended once the production was complete, seemingly the decision of Montand. But it was another nail in the coffin of her marriage to Arthur Miller.

Finally, it was time to start production on *The Misfits*. It was summer of 1960 and a dream team was put together to make the film.

Written by Arthur Miller. Directed by John Huston. And starring, along with Marilyn, Clark Gable, Montgomery Clift and Eli Wallach - all major Hollywood stars.

The film was a major milestone in cinematic history. But as much as Miller had written it for his wife, giving her the kind of role she craved, it did not bring her back to him.

Yet this was not just a spoiled Hollywood star throwing her, very expensive, toys out of the pram. Marilyn was suffering unbelievable internal anxieties.

These came to a head when, towards the end of the summer, she broke down and had to be evacuated to a Los Angeles hospital, where she stayed for ten days receiving extensive psychiatric support.

She returned to filming, but it was a traumatic time for all.

Her relationship with Miller was completely soured. She found some notes he had kept, in which (some claim) he referred to her as a 'whore'.

It all became too much, and long-term happiness eluded her once again. Just prior to the film's premiere, in 1961, Marilyn's third marriage ended.

The Final Scenes

Without Miller's support, he still loved her despite it all, Marilyn's life descended in an ever quicker spiral.

The media response to the news of the Miller's divorce was, unsurprisingly, manic. So keen were they to get a comment, that one journalist thrust his microphone so assertively at Marilyn that it hit her and damaged a tooth.

Then, her co-star and childhood hero – the man she claimed to be her father when a young girl – Clark Gable died from a heart attack. The star had collapsed immediately after filming *The Misfits*, but had appeared to be on the mend.

Next, rumors began that his heart failure had been caused by the stress of working with Marilyn. As ridiculous as this was, it further damaged her mental health, and she swirled into a depressive turmoil.

Perhaps a sign of the love Marilyn inspired, despite the difficulties of living with the woman she had become, was that Joe DiMaggio re-entered her life.

His love for Marilyn had not ended, and he wanted to support her when she was in such a state.

Early in 1961, following the ending of the formal divorce process to Miller, Marilyn entered psychiatric care. When she left – she attended two institutions – a few months later the press demonstrated their usual sensitivity.

They surrounded her, and she needed a police escort to reach her waiting car. As well as her failing mental well-being, physically she was deteriorating fast.

She was hospitalized twice in quick succession, firstly for gynecological problems, then for abdominal troubles.

Matters did improve for a while at the beginning of 1962. She bought a new home – she placed an inscription outside of it – 'Cursom Perficio'. This translates, with an almost unbearable irony, to 'My journey is ending'.

She also received a second Golden Globe in March of 1962. The citation – the world's film favorite.

The next month, she returned to filming – her first movie since *The Misfits*. *Something's Got to Give* was another production for Fox.

Although the studio was sympathetic to its star's condition, and organized filming around her schedule, she was rarely able to attend.

However, she was well enough to travel to New York at the end of May. This was for an enormous celebration to wish President Kennedy happy birthday.

Marilyn had agreed to sing the birthday song. The performance is well known. An especially seductive performance of Happy Birthday.

Few of the many watchers would have known how ill she was.

Fox were angry that she had attended the birthday celebration when she could only rarely attend filming sessions. Shortly after her 36th birthday, she was fired from the film.

Although she had disrupted filming with her regular absence, she had some support on set. Co-star Dean Martin refused to continue without her, and he too was replaced.

During the period from the end of her marriage, there were rumors that Marilyn was having an affair with Frank Sinatra.

Certainly, the two were very close. He bought her a puppy, and she often visited his home.

It was probably through Sinatra that she met President John F Kennedy. At the time, he was campaigning for office. It is widely believed that, during 1961, these two also had an affair.

If true, this would offer some context to her performance of Happy Birthday.

But it seems as though one Kennedy was not enough for Marilyn at this desperate time of her life.

She also had an affair with his younger brother, Robert.

However, such a relationship was dangerous for many reasons. Whilst Attorney General, Kennedy had hunted down organized crime leaders, and revenge was in the air.

It is believed by many that Marilyn's home was bugged, with the crime leaders behind it trying to catch the Kennedy in an uncompromising position with a Hollywood megastar.

Whether true or not, the affair was ended by Robert Kennedy in rapid time.

The last days of Marilyn's life are tricky to decipher.

Some reports say that she fell into a semi-permanent state of drug-induced inertia. Others suggest that she thrilled with the thought of decorating her new home.

Some say that she let her looks slip away, others that she was pleased with a photoshoot she undertook.

August 4th 1962 seemed normal enough, even perhaps better than some of her preceding days.

She spent hours talking to her publicist. She spoke to friends, and was visited by her physician, Dr Greenson, in the late afternoon.

She spoke to Joe DiMaggio's son, and to Marlon Brando. Her friend from the early days, the journalist Sidney Skolsky, was also on her list.

As the night progressed, reports indicated that her speech was becoming slurred. But the mixture of drugs and alcohol to which she regularly turned meant that this was not unusual.

It raised no greater alarm bells than normal.

Sometime that evening, or in the early hours of August 5th, she passed away.

The girl who had grown up without proper parents died alone.

The girl who sought her whole life for somebody who could meet her needs, died with her phone in her hand.

The press even surrounded her body, flashing their cameras wildly, as her body was moved out of her house to the waiting ambulance, and from there to the mortuary.

Her death was officially recorded as 'Probable Suicide', but even in death she could not rest peacefully.

Various theories surfaced to suggest that her demise had been everything from murder to a complete accident.

For years after her death, the Los Angeles Police department was urged to open an investigation into the events of that fateful night.

Robert Slatzer, a former friend who had claimed to be a previous husband, claimed that she had been murdered.

Apparently, she was the victim of an attempt to frame the Kennedy family.

Others felt that she had simply wanted to sleep that night, and had taken too many pills. Some friends felt that she had lost track of the number of pills she had taken, forgetting that she had already had her dose.

A conspiracy theory emerged that she had been killed by the CIA to discredit the Kennedy family.

Poor Marilyn could never be far out of the press and public's imagination.

Having spent a lot of her early career courting public interest, it had come back to haunt her during, even after death.

'A candle in the wind'

Elton John's hit song, *Candle in the Wind*, is one of the most evocative hits of his career. It tells of his fascination for the movie star, how he saw her as 'something more than sexual'.

It was famously adapted for Princess Diana, following her death:

'Goodbye, Norma Jean' transforming to 'Goodbye, England's Rose'.

The lyrics were written by John's writing partner, Bernie Taupin. He points out that the song, whilst making reference to Marilyn Monroe, could be about any star who died young.

But few of those experienced the ups and downs, the media attention and the final fall from grace that the movie star embraced.

There can be few more appropriate descriptions to apply to Marilyn Monroe's life than that she lived it 'like a candle in the wind.'

She never knew who 'to turn to when the rain set in.'

Retrospectively, with our better understanding of mental health, it is hard not to believe that she was particularly susceptible to conditions associated with this illness.

It had plagued her mother, and her grandparents.

Growing up without a father figure, and with constant uncertainty would also have contributed to her emotional fragility.

Then, she was undoubtedly exploited for her looks by the film studios. For someone desperate to be taken seriously for her art, to focus so narrowly on just one of her talents was deeply dispiriting to her.

But for all of this, she did make some great friendships and true loves through her life. The sadness is that she probably rarely recognized this.

But she has left behind a startling legacy. Hers is still one of the most recognized faces in the world, well over fifty years after her death.

Her films remain popular. It is hard, probably impossible, to think of any star, female certainly, to have achieved such a level of fame.

But perhaps most of all, her treatment – along with other great icons such as Princess Diana – should teach us that behind the glamour, there is a person.

A real human being, with loves and dislikes, strengths and weaknesses.

And genuine feelings.

26562622R00078

Made in the USA
Lexington, KY
23 December 2018